The Christmas Crèche

The Christmas Crèche

Elaine Cannon

Featuring nativity scenes from the collection of Holly Zenger

BOOKCRAFT
Salt Lake City, Utah

ISBN 1-57008-574-9

First Printing, 1998

Printed in the United States of America

For unto us a child is born, unto us a son is given . . .

Wonderful, Counsellor, The mighty God . . .

The Prince of Peace.

—Isaiah 9:6

This nativity from Alaska is an Eskimo carving of the holy family in soapstone.

Olmos Hnos. Pujilí — Ecuador

Life HAS BEEN FOREVER BETTER BECAUSE OF THE BIRTH OF THE BABY JESUS IN BETHLEHEM. Annually, an increasing number of Christians lovingly display a nativity scene, or Christmas crèche, in their homes. Often this crèche is handcrafted from local materials, reflecting its native venue. As we share the perspectives of this charming custom through the pages of this book, we recognize common ties among cultures worldwide.

Most people know about Christmas, but what is a Christmas crèche? *Crèche* is French for "crib" or "place of safety," like the manger in which Jesus was placed. Now, universally and reverently, the word *crèche* is used to describe the sacred scene. Key figures encircling the baby Jesus in the manger crib are Mary, Joseph, beasts of burden softened by spring blossoms naming the season, either one angel or a host, a shepherd with a lamb about his shoulders or a flock of sheep around his legs, and exotic Wise Men with their gifts. You'll see that it is a gathering of good company to brighten the celebration of Joy!

*This hand-painted woodcarving is by Olmos Hnas Puiili
in the peasant style of Ecuador.*

Just think, if there *had* been room in the ancient Bethlehem inn, the Holy Child's entry into this mortal world might have been a public show, at best. The inn would have been crowded with guests who had traveled far to this place of their roots to be taxed. Huddled together in the great room, wrapped in their saddle blankets, they would have been privy to the earthly birth of the Son of God!

But there was no room in the inn, so Mary was bedded in the stable. This proved to be a blessing that provided privacy for a woman in labor, with an animal feeding trough, or manger, as a crib for the Baby. With Joseph standing by, behold THE CRÈCHE!

Mexican artisans molded their version of
the first Christmas in local clay.

The Crèche REFLECTS THE CULTURE OF THE LAND WHERE IT IS CREATED— for example, a palm-thatched canopy sheltering a cross-legged manger, a cave behind a plastered khan in the Holy Land, a tall, narrow gable in natural pine from Norway. Key figures in a crèche variously have been made from gnarled olive wood in Jerusalem, multi-grained lumber milled in the Black

Forest of the Bavarian Alps, lacquered papier-mâché, flat silver sheets from Mexico, the same dark heartwood of a South African tree (Diospyros ebenum) used in making black keys of the piano, oriental jade draped with kimonos of silk brocade, clay molded to resemble humble peasants in South America. Though the designs differ, each nativity scene has a heap of straw and a tremulous MARY.

In Bangladesh, the facial features of familiar figures of the nativity, with native details such as a wood pile, roosters, ducks, and an animal stable, are interpreted in soft-sculpture.

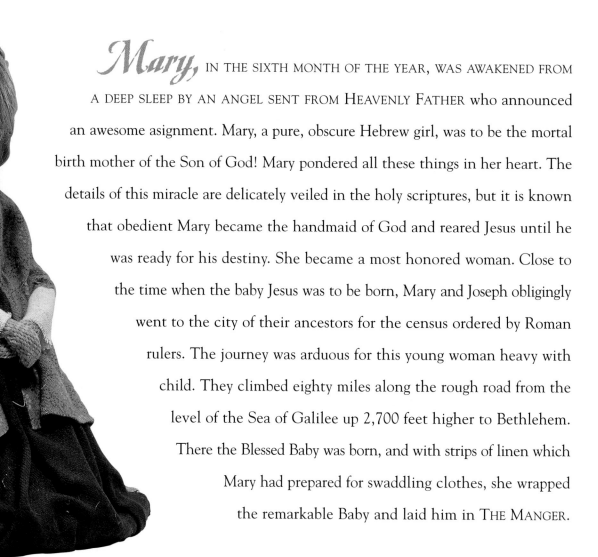

Mary, IN THE SIXTH MONTH OF THE YEAR, WAS AWAKENED FROM A DEEP SLEEP BY AN ANGEL SENT FROM HEAVENLY FATHER who announced an awesome asignment. Mary, a pure, obscure Hebrew girl, was to be the mortal birth mother of the Son of God! Mary pondered all these things in her heart. The details of this miracle are delicately veiled in the holy scriptures, but it is known that obedient Mary became the handmaid of God and reared Jesus until he was ready for his destiny. She became a most honored woman. Close to the time when the baby Jesus was to be born, Mary and Joseph obligingly went to the city of their ancestors for the census ordered by Roman rulers. The journey was arduous for this young woman heavy with child. They climbed eighty miles along the rough road from the level of the Sea of Galilee up 2,700 feet higher to Bethlehem. There the Blessed Baby was born, and with strips of linen which Mary had prepared for swaddling clothes, she wrapped the remarkable Baby and laid him in THE MANGER.

Coarse, peasant burlap and fiber twine make up this nativity created in a German village.

The Manger WAS INDEED A HUMBLE PLACE TO LAY THE HOLY CHILD WHO WAS TO BE KING OF KINGS!
Yet all about the stable were his own godly creations—lilies of the field, reeds and rushes, the early-blooming pink
almond buds (*almond* means "the waker" in Hebrew), and the desert rose that became the poet's metaphor:

Lo, how a Rose e'er blooming

From tender stem hath sprung!

Of Jesse's lineage coming

As men of old have sung.

It came a flow'ret bright,

Amid the cold of winter,

When half spent was the night.

Isaiah 'twas foretold it,

The Rose I have in mind,

With Mary we behold it,

The virgin mother kind.

To show God's love aright,

She bore to men a Savior,

When half spent was the night.

—16th-century carol

There, too,
resting in cool
grasses and
curling vines,
were God's
creatures—
THE ANIMALS.

*The black holy
family depicted in
this crèche from
Zululand, Southeast
Africa, is dressed in
native costumes of
beads and beans.*

Shepherds tenderly worship the holy family in this stark scene from the desert people of Arabia.

Shepherds STILL LEAD THEIR SHEEP ACROSS A FIELD OUTSIDE BETHLEHEM. Sheep still safely graze near a Bedouin tent. The image is complete with jingling bells on the lead sheep and the flock following its shepherd, who is clothed in the traditional desert robes of his work. (Sometimes his turban is green, marking the man as a descendant of Muhammad.) On that holy night two thousand years ago, in the same country, there were shepherds abiding in the field east of the plateau that is Bethlehem, keeping watch over their flocks against creatures of prey.

Darkness—only the light of stars.

Stillness—only the distant wail of a howling wolf.

Suddenly an angel of the Lord appeared to the shepherds, and the glory of the Lord shone round about them. The angel gave the glad news of the birth of the Christ Child! The sign given for finding the Christ Child was that he would be a babe wrapped in swaddling clothes, lying in a manger.

The shepherds heard this news in joy and saw the scene with eyes of faith. When they found the holy family they spread the exciting news abroad, telling it on the mountain, saying everything that had been made known to them by THE ANGEL.

The Star! THE STAR! The brilliant Star of Bethlehem was recognized by the Wise Men as the sign that had been foretold. They also knew they were to follow that miraculous guiding Star to find him who was born King of the Jews. According to tradition, that Star was brighter than any other, dimming the sparkle of the diamond-riddled heaven. It danced across the skies before the Wise Men until it stood over the place where the young child was. The Wise Men rejoiced with exceeding great joy, for that Star had taken them to the Holy Baby who was guarded by JOSEPH.

Carved of olive wood in Israel, this crèche has a moving star that marks the place where Jesus was.

"*Joseph,* THOU SON OF DAVID," SAID THE ANGEL, "fear not to take unto thee Mary thy wife: for that which is conceived in her is of the Holy Ghost." Joseph had spent a restless night after he learned about Mary's being pregnant before their marriage. What a situation! But the angel comforted him and commanded Joseph that he should name the child "Jesus: for he shall save his people from their sins." Joseph did as the angel of the Lord had bidden him. Later the angel came again to Joseph, warning him to take Mary and Jesus to Egypt to escape harm from Herod's massacre of infants in Bethlehem. When Herod was safely dead, the angel reappeared to Joseph, telling him to move the family back to Nazareth. Though Joseph, the son of Heli, was considered a fine man, he was known to be poor. At the presentation of Jesus in the temple, he took only two turtle doves instead of the more costly offering of a sacrificial lamb. Joseph was regarded as a proper father according to the Hebrew tradition, providing for the child in every way. And he taught the carpenter's trade to JESUS.

This museum-quality crèche was handcarved by the gifted sculptor G. Lama, and shows Mary lifting the swaddling clothes to reveal the baby Jesus.

$\mathcal{J}\mathit{esus},$ BORN IN A STABLE IN BETHLEHEM, nonetheless grew and waxed strong in wisdom and favor with God and man. In every category of humanity he was *the* mighty factor in the history of the world. He was the one perfect man in whom the world has never found a fault, nor does he have an equal. Whether people know it yet or not, that baby Jesus born in a stable *was* the Son of God the Father! He is Christ, the Savior of mankind, which is why the heavenly hosts sang glad tidings of great joy. Now a sacred symbol of that promise unto all people is the CHRISTMAS CRÈCHE.

This Italian bisque nativity with sterling silver crowns, lantern, and gifts of the Magi, is notable because of the Victorian period nightcap on the head of baby Jesus.

The Christmas Crèche IS A WONDER. Though the sacred subject is the same, there is infinite variety through the perspective of each artisan, their creations becoming type and shadow for all. People can be obedient like Mary, be defenders of Christ like Joseph, share the good news like angels, humbly seek the Lord like the shepherds, go great lengths to bring gifts like the Wise Men. Also, filled with the glowing Spirit of God, they can guide others to Christ like the Star of Bethlehem!

Jesus was born unto all people, in all places, in all times. He loves us and invites everyone to come unto him! Jesus said, "Love one another; as I have loved you." Even if we *seem* different from each other, we are the same to Christ. We, too, are to love all of God's children. Surely this kind of love is the miracle of the Christmas Crèche, with its gathering of good company, all peaceable followers of Christ bound together to brighten the season!

This collage is a reminder of the wondrous birth of Jesus and the loving lessons he taught mankind. This gathering of good company from worldwide artists includes scenes from Bangladesh, Germany, Laos, Arabia, France, Israel, and Italy.

Acknowledgments

A wondrous aura pervades a community where people not only have reverence for life but love each other. During the Creation, God said, "Let there be light." With that Light we see the value of our relationship with him and with others. We help each other believe in God, the Heavenly Father of us all, and we praise him. Across the world people preserve the tender traditions celebrating the birth of God's Only Begotten Son in the flesh. These feelings are artistically expressed as the Light is given them, compatible with their community heritage. Examples of such glorious work are pictured in this significant book.

Surely with others I acknowledge these artisans. I express gratitude for the inimitable help from the scientific research, scripture scholarship, and the artistic and insightful skills of Susan McOmber and Carla Cannon. I also extend thanks for the photography by John Luke, as well as the production efforts of Jana Erickson, Janna DeVore, Cory Maxwell, and Brad Pelo of Bookcraft.

Elaine Cannon